HOW TO WRITE A COMPELLING RESUME AND COVER LETTER

Rules, Tips and Essential Elements

Robert L. White Ph.D

ABOUT THE AUTHOR

Dr. Robert L. White is a distinguished author, entrepreneur, and expert in Business and Human Resources management. With a wealth of experience and academic prowess, Dr. White has positioned himself as a thought leader in the field, offering valuable insights to individuals seeking success in their professional journeys.

Dr. Robert L. White has earned a Ph.D. in Business and Human Resources management, showcasing a commitment to academic excellence and a deep understanding of the intricate dynamics of business operations and human capital management.

At the helm of a successful business, Dr. White has demonstrated an exemplary ability to navigate the complexities of the business world. His leadership has undoubtedly played a pivotal role in the growth and prosperity of the enterprise.

In addition to his role in the business sector, Dr. White holds significant positions as both the Board Chairman and a distinguished member of multinational recruiting firms. This dual role affords him a unique perspective, combining leadership at the strategic level with hands-on involvement in the recruitment industry.

Dr. White's expertise lies at the intersection of business strategy and human resources management. His profound knowledge in these areas is not only reflected in his academic achievements but is also evident in the success of the business he leads and his contributions to multinational recruiting firms.

As the author of the book "How to Answer Job Interview Questions: Easy and Comprehensive Step-by-Step Guide to Landing a Job," Dr. White extends his expertise to a broader audience. The book is a testament to his commitment to empowering individuals with the knowledge and skills needed to navigate the competitive landscape of job interviews successfully.

Beyond his entrepreneurial endeavors, Dr. White's roles as the Board Chairman and a member of multinational recruiting firms underscore his commitment to shaping the future of the business landscape. These leadership positions position him as a key influencer in decision-making processes at both organizational and industry levels.

In his multifaceted career, Dr. Robert L. White has not only demonstrated a keen understanding of the intricacies of business and human resources but has actively contributed to the growth and development of individuals and organizations alike. His leadership, academic achievements, and authorship collectively paint a portrait of an individual dedicated to fostering success and excellence in the professional realm.

Table of Contents

INTRODUCTION

A well-written CV and cover letter are crucial in the maze-like current job market, where opportunities are hard to come by and competition is intense. These two documents function as your first point of contact with potential employers, allowing you to create a strong impression that might lead to your ideal position.

In this book, "How to Write a Compelling Resume and Cover Letter: Rules, Tips, and Essential Elements," we will travel through the complex craft of writing a resume and cover letter in this extensive guide, covering the core ideas, industry best practices, and cutting-edge tactics required to make a lasting impression in the competitive job market of today.

Understanding the Importance of Resumes and Cover Letters:
In the first few chapters, we will discuss the importance of resumes and cover letters in the hiring process. We will examine why the first impression they give can make or break your chances of success as we unlock the riddles around their function as gatekeepers to career possibilities.

We will examine how these documents function as effective tools for drawing in hiring managers and landing desired interviews, from emphasizing your abilities and experiences to exhibiting your personality and excitement.

Navigating the Landscape of Modern Job Applications:

As we go along, we'll examine the structure of a successful resume, dissecting its fundamental elements and assisting you in customizing it for particular job openings. Regardless of your experience level and career goals, we will offer advice on how to choose the best resume style, measure your accomplishments, and create an engaging story that will catch the attention of potential employers.

The Role of Resumes in Job Applications

Resumes remain the standard document that connects job seekers and potential employers in the huge world of job applications. They operate as the initial point of contact and provide a first look into the professional lives of applicants contending for positions that are highly sought after in the current competitive job market.

Significance of Cover Letters in the Hiring Process

Within the ever-changing realm of job applications, cover letters prove to be invaluable allies for resumes, providing candidates with a singular chance to delve deeper into their professional identities and go beyond the bullet points. Although resumes give a brief overview of a candidate's experiences and credentials, cover letters function as individualized narratives that shed light on the candidate's goals, motivations, and fit for the position.

Applying a cover letter allows candidates to add individuality and authenticity to their application, something that resumes typically don't allow. With the help of their platform, job seekers may establish personal connections with hiring managers and share viewpoints, tales, and anecdotes that are difficult to communicate through a résumé.

Demonstrating a sincere interest in the position and organization to which the applicant is applying is one of the main purposes of a cover letter. Candidates can stand out from the crowd of applications by clearly communicating their grasp of the company's vision, values, and culture, as well as their excitement and passion for the opportunity.

Candidates might additionally address certain demands and problems mentioned in the job description in their cover letters. Through cover letters, candidates can customize their applications to the specific requirements of the role and firm, whether that be emphasizing relevant experiences, addressing potential concerns, or coming up with innovative solutions to urgent problems.

In almost every professional context, the ability to communicate effectively is essential, and cover letters give applicants a chance to demonstrate their written communication abilities. Candidates can use cover letters to show that they can communicate succinctly, clearly, and effectively by using them to develop engaging introductory paragraphs and articulate strong arguments in favor of their candidacies.

The First Impression: Why it Matters

A CV is more than just a summary of one's education and work history; it is a picture of one's professional identity, a narrative that has been thoughtfully chosen to make an impact on hiring managers. An effective CV is crucial in a world where people's attention spans are short and first impressions count for a lot.

We will tie up the loose ends of our journey in the last few chapters, providing parting advice for success and inspiration for job seekers starting their own paths to professional satisfaction. "How to Write a Compelling Resume and Cover Letter" is a reliable guide that will help you achieve your goals with clarity, insight, and steadfast support, regardless of where you are in your career or how you are starting out.

Without further ado, let's start this life-changing adventure together and discover the techniques for crafting cover letters and resumes that grab readers' attention motivate them to take action, and lead to a world of opportunities.

CHAPTER 1

RESUME ESSENTIALS

One document that is frequently utilized in the employment process is a résumé. It contains details about your experience and education and ought to convey to potential employers the most pertinent and significant facts about you in an understandable manner. The objective is to succinctly convey how your experiences and skill set make you uniquely qualified for the r
ole.

Any job seeker hoping to leave a lasting impression on potential employers must create a compelling resume. A cohesive and eye-catching CV acts as a road map for your career, succinctly and effectively summarizing your abilities, experiences, and credentials.

Anatomy of a Winning Resume

A strong resume does more than just sum up your education and experience; it skillfully tells the tale of your professional journey in a way that grabs the attention of hiring managers and persuades them that you are the right candidate. Below is a summary of the essential elements that constitute a successful resume:

Name and Method of Contact
Your name ought to be the first thing an employer sees on your CV. Make sure the writing for your name is bold and larger. After your name, put your credentials and leave off prefixes like Mr. or Ms.

If you are applying for a creative position, for instance, you may also add a link to your online portfolio.

A strong CV makes it clear to potential employers how to get in touch with you. Make sure your contact information is at the bottom of your resume so a potential employer doesn't have to read the entire document. Just underneath your name on the résumé, include your contact details. Additionally, since certain ATSs are unable to read information found in headers or footers, you should refrain from including important information like contact details in these sections.

Resume Summary or Objective

You might choose to insert an objective statement or resume summary after your contact details. If you have little professional experience, like most recent college or high school graduates, an objective statement is a suitable option because it offers a concise explanation of your career ambitions. A resume summary is a succinct paragraph that highlights your relevant work experience and talents using action verbs.

Professional Summary

A strong summary statement is an essential component of any outstanding resume. A resume summary should consist of two to four sentences that showcase your most relevant experiences, certifications, talents, and other qualities. Make sure you highlight your contribution to the success of your organization with one or more quantifiable accomplishments.

It ought to contain the following:

A succinct summary of your experiences, major competencies, and professional goals at the start of your resume.

Customize your professional summary for the job for which you are applying, emphasizing how your experience meets the needs of the role.

It should be succinct and compelling, with an emphasis on what you can do for the employer.

Section on Skills

Include a table of your most important hard and soft skill sets at the start of your resume to save recruiters from having to search for the most important information. Make sure the abilities you've emphasized demonstrate your suitability for the position; it would be ideal if these were keywords from the job description.

We must first clarify the distinction between the two primary categories of skills—soft and hard—before we can begin this section.

Hard Skills

In layman's terms, a hard skill is not industry-specific and can be taught, developed, or tested.
These include language proficiency, computer proficiency, and heavy machinery operation.

Soft Skills

A soft skill is an intangible personality attribute that enhances one's performance at work but is difficult to quantify.

These abilities include things like having a positive attitude, being motivated to succeed, and playing well in a team.

Having identified both categories of skills, the choice of which to list on your CV is essentially yours.

It is crucial that you list them so that the hiring manager can quickly review and take note of them.

They are far more likely to consider your CV if they can tell right away that you possess the talents they are looking for.

In conclusion, emphasize your most important, job-relevant talents and competencies.

Sort skills into groups based on things like spoken languages, software expertise, and technical skills.
Incorporate both hard and soft skills (e.g., leadership, communication, programming languages, project management).

Employment History
The core of your resume is your work experience.
The hiring manager would start by looking through your job titles and previous employers. Make sure it's simple to locate this information.

This section's fundamentals ought to comprise:
Job position
Company
Location of the Company
Dates of employment

However, even if your job history is remarkable and can be condensed into these four areas, it could not be sufficient for the company.
Employers are far more interested in the impact you have on the businesses you previously worked for than they are in basic information.

Both outcomes and numbers are significant. When demonstrating influence, use action verbs and quantify accomplishments (e.g., "Increased sales by 20%").

Whatever your past roles were, there's always a metric that can demonstrate to a prospective employer that you made a big difference.

Education

Your resume must include a clear education section, particularly if you recently graduated or have little professional experience.

If your academic record is strong and you don't have much work experience, you might want to consider including all of your educational achievements in a very extensive education section.

On the other hand, your education section should only provide the bare minimum if you have a few years of job experience.

Generally, it would be sufficient to include the name of the school, the years of attendance, and your degree.

Additional Sections (Awards, Certifications, etc.)

You already know everything you need to know for your resume if you've read this far.

If you believe they would be helpful in any way, or if you feel your resume is still lacking something, you can add a couple of extra sections.

Credentials, Honors, and Awards
If you choose to pursue this part, you should be prepared to present something truly noteworthy, since it has the potential to be highly significant.

Make sure you know which certificates to include in your CV before sending it if your prospective employer requests to view them. If you omit any, it could damage your application by giving the impression that you lack the necessary experience.

In all other cases, feel free to include any certifications, honors, or awards you believe are pertinent to your CV.

Also feel free to add any other section such as listed below that you beleive would give you an advantage in the hiring process.
Projects
Hobbies & Interests
Publications
Volunteering.

CHAPTER 2

CHOOSING THE RIGHT RESUME FORMAT

Selecting the appropriate resume format is essential because it affects how prospective employers will see your abilities, experiences, and credentials. There are various formats available, each suited to the requirements of job seekers in varying industries and career stages. The most popular resume formats and their attributes are shown below:

CHRONOLOGICAL RESUME

A chronological resume begins with your most recent employment and highlights your accomplishments, then details your prior positions in reverse chronological order. The chronological resume is the best option for job seekers who have a ton of experience and accomplishments to include in their resume for just this reason.

Most importantly, research indicates that recruiters also prefer chronological resumes.

Why? A recruiter will be looking for work experience on your resume because you are seeking a job.
But fear not—even as a recent graduate, you can chronologically organize your resume. You may also choose from other widely used formats that better suit your needs.

Structure of a Chronological Resume
A simple format is followed by a chronological resume. All that matters is that your most recent or current experience, whether it be academic or professional, should come first. Then comes the second most recent, and so forth.

The primary and most widely used sections of a chronological resume structure are as follows:
Contact Information

Professional title, objective, and summary for resume
Experience at work and accomplishments

Section on Education
Your strongest hard and soft skills
Add any optional parts you choose (languages, certifications, volunteer work, etc.).

You still have the option to create your resume using a chronological layout if you're a recent college graduate.

All you need to do is flip the sections of your resume around so that your education section appears first.

You're set to go here as well. Just make sure that your schooling entries are arranged from most recent to least recent.

Example 1: Chronological Resume for Experienced Professional
[Full Name]
[Address]
[City, State, Zip Code]
[Phone Number]
[Email Address]
[LinkedIn Profile]

Professional Summary:
Dedicated and results-driven marketing manager with over 10 years of experience in developing and implementing strategic marketing campaigns. Proven track record of driving revenue growth through innovative marketing strategies and effective team leadership. Skilled in market research, brand management, and digital marketing techniques.

Skills:
Strategic Planning
Brand Development
Market Research & Analysis
Digital Marketing
Team Leadership
Project Management
Budget Management

Social Media Marketing
Work Experience:
Marketing Manager
XYZ Corporation, Town, USA
[Month, Year] - Present

Developed and executed comprehensive marketing strategies to increase brand visibility and drive sales growth.

Led a team of marketing professionals in the creation and implementation of integrated marketing campaigns across digital and traditional channels.

Conducted market research and analysis to identify emerging trends and opportunities for product expansion.
Managed marketing budgets and allocated resources effectively to maximize ROI.

Oversaw the development of marketing collateral, including brochures, presentations, and advertisements.
Cultivated relationships with key stakeholders, including clients, vendors, and media partners.

Senior Marketing Specialist
ABC Company, Anytown, USA
[Month, Year] - [Month, Year]

Managed all aspects of marketing campaigns, from concept development to execution and analysis.

Implemented social media marketing strategies to increase brand engagement and drive website traffic.

Conducted competitive analysis and market research to inform marketing strategies and tactics.

Collaborated with cross-functional teams to develop and launch new products and promotions.

Tracked and analyzed campaign performance metrics to measure effectiveness and identify areas for improvement.

Education:
Bachelor of Business Administration in Marketing
University of XYZ, Anytown, USA
[Month, Year] - [Month, Year]
Certifications:
Google Ads Certification
HubSpot Inbound Marketing Certification
Example 2: Chronological Resume for Recent Graduate
[Full Name]
[Address]
[City, State, Zip Code]
[Phone Number]
[Email Address]
[LinkedIn Profile]

Professional Summary:
Motivated and detail-oriented recent graduate with a Bachelor of Science in Computer Science. Solid foundation in programming languages, software development, and database management. Eager to apply academic knowledge and gain practical experience in a software development role.

Skills:
Programming Languages: Java, Python, C++
Web Development: HTML, CSS, JavaScript
Database Management: SQL
Software Development Lifecycle
Problem-solving
Team Collaboration
Attention to Detail
Work Experience:
Internship - Software Development
DEF Corporation, Anytown, USA
[Month, Year] - [Month, Year]

Assisted in the development and testing of software applications under the guidance of senior developers.

Participated in team meetings and contributed to project discussions and planning sessions.
Conducted troubleshooting and debugging to identify and resolve software issues.
Documented software features, functionalities, and bugs for future reference.

Education:
Bachelor of Science in Computer Science
University of ABC, Anytown, USA
[Month, Year] - [Month, Year]

Projects:
Developed a web-based inventory management system using Java, HTML, CSS, and MySQL for a final year project.

Created a mobile app prototype for task management using Android Studio and Java.

Certifications:
Oracle Certified Associate, Java SE 8 Programmer
Microsoft Technology Associate: Database Fundamentals

FUNCTIONAL RESUME

A functional resume, sometimes referred to as a skill-based resume, emphasizes your professional skills over your employment history.

In a functional resume, you state all of your talents and then include examples of how you've used them in the real world to support them. In a traditional resume, your work experience is listed in reverse chronological order.
When should I utilize a functional CV?

In the following scenarios, a functional resume is preferable:

You recently graduated and have never had a job. The functional resume can be highly beneficial to students because it places more emphasis on skills than experience.
You're going to change careers. You can use a functional resume to emphasize how your talents make you the best candidate if you have some work experience, but it isn't relevant to the position you're going for.

You've experienced lengthy periods of unemployment. You can utilize the functional resume format to minimize the gaps in your work history because it emphasizes skills over experience.

That being stated, we do not advise using a functional resume in around 90% of circumstances.

There are benefits to it, such as being noticed as a fresh graduate, but there are also serious drawbacks.

Firstly, the functional resume format is not nearly as well-known as the traditional one, and in some regions of the world, recruiters may not even be aware that it exists.

Furthermore, the absence of work experience on a resume may raise red flags with some recruiters, suggesting that the applicant isn't telling the truth (e.g., red flags, being fired from previous employment, etc.).

Together, these two drawbacks provide strong evidence against the functional resume style.

Therefore, consider the advantages and disadvantages and proceed at your own risk if you decide to develop a functional resume!

Below is an example of a functional resume tailored for a job seeker with a diverse skill set and relevant experiences, ideal for someone transitioning between industries or addressing employment gaps:

[Full Name]
[Address]
[City, State, Zip Code]

[Phone Number]
[Email Address]
[LinkedIn Profile]

Professional Summary:
Results-oriented professional with a diverse background in project management, customer service, and administrative support. Proven ability to manage multiple projects simultaneously, deliver exceptional customer experiences, and streamline operational processes. Skilled in problem-solving, communication, and collaboration. Seeking opportunities to leverage my transferable skills in a new industry.

Skills:

Project Management
Customer Relationship Management
Administrative Support
Team Leadership
Process Improvement
Data Analysis
Time Management
Communication Skills
Experience Highlights:

Project Manager
XYZ Consulting, Anytown, USA
[Month, Year] - Present

Led cross-functional teams in the planning and execution of projects, ensuring adherence to timelines and budgets.

Developed project plans, schedules, and milestones to track progress and ensure successful project delivery.

Facilitated communication between team members, clients, and stakeholders to address concerns and resolve issues.

Conducted risk assessments and implemented mitigation strategies to minimize project risks and maximize outcomes.

Prepared and delivered project status reports and presentations to management and key stakeholders.
Customer Service Representative
ABC Corporation, Anytown, USA
[Month, Year] - [Month, Year]

Provided exceptional customer service and support to clients via phone, email, and in-person interactions.
Resolved customer inquiries, complaints, and escalations in a timely and professional manner, exceeding customer expectations.

Identified opportunities to improve customer service processes and implemented solutions to enhance efficiency and effectiveness.

Collaborated with cross-functional teams to address customer needs and achieve business objectives.
Administrative Assistant
DEF Company, Anytown, USA
[Month, Year] - [Month, Year]

Supported executive team members with administrative tasks, including calendar management, travel arrangements, and expense reporting.

Coordinated meetings, conferences, and events, handling logistics and ensuring seamless execution.

Managed office operations, including inventory management, supply ordering, and vendor relations.
Created and maintained organizational systems and processes to optimize workflow and productivity.

Education:
Bachelor of Arts in Business Administration
University of XYZ, Anytown, USA
[Month, Year] - [Month, Year]

Certifications:

Project Management Professional (PMP)
Customer Service Excellence Certification

Additional Information:
Fluent in Spanish
Volunteer Experience: Community Outreach Program Coordinator, Anytown Nonprofit Organization

This functional resume example emphasizes the candidate's transferable skills and experiences relevant to the desired position, while downplaying specific job titles or employment dates. It effectively showcases the candidate's qualifications and suitability for roles in various industries.

COMBINATION RESUME

There is a hybrid resume, also known as a combination resume, which falls somewhere between the more contemporary functional resume and the conventional chronological resume. When a candidate's professional qualities are not properly conveyed by either the chronological or functional style, they typically adopt the combination approach.

A combination resume creates a unique format by combining some aspects of a functional resume and some components of a chronological resume. Keep in mind that whilst your functional resume puts your talents front and center, your chronological resume is structured around your employment history.

Usually, this entails giving a thorough account of your professional background and the particular abilities you've acquired over time. There are, nevertheless, various ways to display this data. This adaptable framework is dependent on the narrative you wish to convey.

When to utilize a combined resume

For those who desire a resume that highlights their talents and is optimized for automatic tracking system (ATS) scanning, a combo resume can be a smart choice.

If your desired position does not quite match the job titles you have had, you might wish to highlight your skills on your resume. You might think about writing a combo resume, for instance, if you are looking for a position at the entry-level making the switch to a new profession or sector aiming for professional progress

Although you can (and should!) include your accomplishments and talents in your work experience section, having a separate skills section will assist you show that you have applied the advanced abilities employers are seeking in ways that go beyond your prior job duties.

Concerning the second requirement, you should normally choose an ATS-friendly structure unless you are sending your resume directly to a recruiter. If you apply for a job via a corporate website, you can generally assume that your resume will be "read" by an automated technology system (ATS) before a human recruiter does.

The majority of Applicant Tracking Systems are designed to scan chronological resumes, looking for pertinent job histories, job titles, and keywords related to vacant positions. The ATS may view individuals who submit functional resumes as lacking the work history necessary for a position since functional resumes frequently lack the job history details that many ATS check for.

But when you create a combination resume, you usually format your job history according to the best practices of the applicant tracking system (ATS) while providing more information about your improved skill set for the recruiter who will review your resume after it passes the ATS scan. Format for a combination resume

Although the format of the combo resume is variable, it must include at least the following sections:

Header
Skills
Work history
Some optional sections that could be included are:
Summary or goal?
Learning
Credentials
Initiatives
Volunteer work
Hobby

Before choosing which sections to include and what order to present them, consider the narrative you want to tell and the essential details you must provide. The format that works best for your story can then be pieced together from there.

Below is an example of a combination resume tailored for a job seeker with both relevant work experience and strong skills, ideal for highlighting achievements and qualifications while showcasing transferable skills:

[Full Name]
[Address]
[City, State, Zip Code]
[Phone Number]
[Email Address]
[LinkedIn Profile]

Professional Summary:

Results-driven professional with over 5 years of experience in project management and team leadership. Proven track record of delivering successful projects on time and within budget. Skilled in strategic planning, problem-solving, and cross-functional collaboration. Strong communicator with the ability to motivate teams and drive results.

Skills:

Project Management
Team Leadership
Strategic Planning
Budget Management
Risk Assessment & Mitigation
Stakeholder Engagement
Problem-solving
Cross-functional Collaboration
Communication Skills
Microsoft Project, Excel, PowerPoint
Work Experience:

Project Manager
ABC Corporation, Anytown, USA
[Month, Year] - Present

Led cross-functional teams in the planning, execution, and delivery of complex projects, ensuring alignment with business objectives.
Developed project plans, schedules, and budgets, and monitored progress to ensure adherence to timelines and financial targets.

Conducted risk assessments and implemented mitigation strategies to minimize project risks and maximize outcomes.

Facilitated communication and collaboration between team members, clients, and stakeholders to drive project success.

Prepared and delivered project status reports and presentations to senior management and key stakeholders.
Operations Coordinator
DEF Company, Anytown, USA
[Month, Year] - [Month, Year]

Managed day-to-day operations of the organization, overseeing administrative tasks, budgeting, and resource allocation.

Developed and implemented operational policies and procedures to streamline workflow and improve efficiency.
Collaborated with department heads to identify opportunities for process improvement and implement solutions.
Conducted data analysis to evaluate operational performance and identify areas for optimization.

Provided training and support to staff members to ensure compliance with operational standards and best practices.

Education:
Bachelor of Science in Business Administration
University of XYZ, Anytown, USA

[Month, Year] - [Month, Year]

Certifications:

Project Management Professional (PMP)
Six Sigma Green Belt Certification
Additional Information:

Volunteer Experience: Project Management Mentor, Anytown Nonprofit Organization

Languages: Fluent in Spanish and proficient in French

This combination resume effectively showcases the candidate's relevant work experience, skills, and qualifications. By combining a detailed summary of accomplishments with a comprehensive skills section, this format allows the candidate to highlight their achievements while emphasizing their transferable skills and qualifications.

TARGETED RESUME

Writing a CV specifically for a job opportunity is known as targeting. It emphasizes the qualifications and experience that are pertinent to that role. You should modify your CV for each job application to make it more pertinent to that particular role. When you demonstrate that you have the knowledge and expertise needed for the position, you stand a better chance of being invited for an interview.

Below is an example of a targeted resume tailored for a specific job or industry, emphasizing the candidate's relevant experiences, skills, and achievements that directly align with the requirements of the desired position:

[Full Name]
[Address]
[City, State, Zip Code]
[Phone Number]
[Email Address]
[LinkedIn Profile]

Professional Summary:
Results-oriented marketing professional with extensive experience in digital marketing and brand management. Proven track record of driving revenue growth through strategic marketing initiatives and effective campaign management. Skilled in market analysis, audience segmentation, and brand positioning. Seeking to leverage my expertise in digital marketing to drive growth and innovation in a dynamic marketing role.

Skills:

Digital Marketing Strategy
Social Media Marketing
Content Creation & Management
Search Engine Optimization (SEO)
Email Marketing
Data Analytics & Reporting
Brand Development & Positioning
Market Research & Analysis
Project Management
Adobe Creative Suite
Work Experience:

Digital Marketing Manager
ABC Tech Solutions, Anytown, USA
[Month, Year] - Present

Developed and executed comprehensive digital marketing strategies to increase brand visibility and drive lead generation.

Managed all aspects of digital marketing campaigns, including social media, email marketing, and content creation.

Conducted market research and competitor analysis to identify trends and opportunities for growth.

Analyzed campaign performance metrics and KPIs to optimize marketing strategies and drive ROI.
Collaborated with cross-functional teams to develop and launch new products and initiatives.

Social Media Specialist
ABC Marketing Agency, Anytown, USA
[Month, Year] - [Month, Year]

Managed social media accounts for clients across various industries, creating engaging content and driving brand awareness.

Developed and implemented social media strategies to increase follower engagement and drive website traffic.

Monitored social media channels for customer inquiries and feedback, responding promptly to maintain positive brand reputation.

Analyzed social media metrics and performance data to track campaign effectiveness and inform future strategy.

Education:
Bachelor of Business Administration in Marketing
University of XYZ, Anytown, USA
[Month, Year] - [Month, Year]

Certifications:
Google Ads Certification
HubSpot Inbound Marketing Certification
Facebook Blueprint Certification

Additional Information:
Volunteer Experience: Marketing Committee Member, Local Nonprofit Organization

Portfolio: Link to online portfolio showcasing digital marketing campaigns and projects

This targeted resume is tailored specifically for a marketing role, highlighting the candidate's relevant experiences, skills, and certifications related to digital marketing. By focusing on achievements and qualifications directly relevant to the desired position, this resume effectively demonstrates the candidate's suitability and expertise for the job.

Take into account industry standards, your career level, and the particulars of the position you're applying for when selecting the format for your resume. Format your CV to effectively present your abilities, accomplishments, and credentials while facilitating hiring managers' quick comprehension of your work history.

CHAPTER 3

TAILORING YOUR RESUME TO SPECIFIC JOBS

To increase your chances of getting interviews and eventually getting the desired position, you must customize your resume for each job that you apply for. Relevant professional work experience is either required or strongly preferred in over 80% of job advertisements. An employer can see from a customized resume that you possess the abilities they are looking for and have demonstrated success using them in the past.

This implies that the job description on your CV must include the information the recruiting manager is seeking. You won't be invited for an interview if it doesn't.

The issue is that the majority of job searchers just draft one resume, which they include with each application. Although it saves time, it's doubtful that your CV will meet the requirements of every job you apply to.

You must customize your resume for each opportunity if you want to receive more job interviews.

BENEFITS OF TAILORING YOUR RESUME
Having a CV that is specifically designed for you will help you stand out from the competition and increase your chances of being invited for an interview. These are some of the causes:

It demonstrates your alignment with the job.
You exhibit a track record of carrying out comparable obligations by emphasizing your most pertinent experiences and abilities.

It proves your interest.
Because you take the additional time and care to make sure your resume highlights your best-fit qualifications, tailoring it can demonstrate your sincere interest in the position. Employing managers will value this consideration and be more enthusiastic about a prospect who appears ready to work for them.

It emphasizes the employer's needs.
Hiring managers are looking for candidates who can help them achieve their objectives. Emphasizing your most useful abilities and noteworthy achievements demonstrates to them that you are thinking about their needs as well as what the job can do for you.

It can help you pass applicant tracking systems.
These tools are often used by hiring managers nowadays to sift through resumes based on keywords included in the job description. Your chances of getting your resume read will increase if you customize it based on the job description.

CUSTOMIZING FOR JOB DESCRIPTIONS
Customizing job duties is known as "job customization," or "job carving" in some cases. It is a method of maximizing the abilities and skills of workers with disabilities while increasing employee productivity by mixing duties from several jobs. The main idea of job carving is to create a new position by relieving specialist workers of non-specialized responsibilities.

Why take the action?
To boost service delivery, business profitability, and the production time of specialist workers.

How does it operate?
To improve services and boost profitability, the employer and service provider collaborate to find opportunities.

From the standpoint of the service provider
Finding employment duties in an environment that is tailored to a prospective new employee with a disability's requirements, capacities, skills, abilities, and aptitudes is the key.

From the Employer's Perspective

Finding non-specialized duties carried out by specialized workers is the key to creating a new, relevant position that can be filled by a different individual.

Perspective of a New Employee
A fresh, customized job description that matches the abilities and capabilities of a potential hire is created through the job customization process. It provides a disabled job seeker with the chance to contribute by their abilities.

JOB CARVING – JOB CUSTOMIZATION – CUSTOMIZED EMPLOYMENT

A customized job offer is based on an assessment of the candidate's suitability for the position and the needs of the company. Tailored solutions are designed to benefit all parties involved, and effective job carving benefits specialized workers, employers, and job seekers.

Highlighting Relevant Experience

Companies search for applicants whose credentials meet their requirements for open positions. Employing managers evaluate applicant resumes to determine which candidates are qualified for a position based on their professional experiences and pertinent abilities. Relevant experience lets you highlight your qualifications for jobs, no matter what your professional background is. This article defines relevant experience, goes over some important pointers for choosing experiences to highlight on your CV, and provides a list of real-world examples to get you started on creating your own.

What is relevant experience?

Any professional work experience that qualifies you for a particular position is considered relevant experience. Even if a candidate lacks expertise in their field, employers can learn a great deal about their potential contributions from resumes that highlight related experiences.

Advice on how to find and include relevant experience

You can make sure that your prior work responsibilities and skill set match the positions you wish to pursue in a few different ways. The following advice may help you find relevant experiences to highlight on your targeted resume:

Review the job description

You should start by reviewing the original job description for the position you wish to seek to find experiences that might be relevant. Emphasize pertinent abilities, duties, or educational needs; alternatively, take the time to record them in writing so that they can be compared later. This makes you consider what you can offer an employer and whether you are now eligible for a job.

Examine the job description and the qualifications listed on your existing resume.

Evaluate your qualifications against an employer's requirements by comparing them to the job description and your most recent resume. To accomplish this, make a chart and list the number of ways in which what you can provide and what the employer needs differ. You can then focus your resume's highlights on the most relevant aspects of that specific job position.

In the areas of abilities and professional background, highlight pertinent experiences.
The primary places where you can showcase your relevant experiences are in the sections on your professional experiences and skills. Begin by looking over each component and marking out any accomplishment, duty, or skill that doesn't directly contribute to the job at hand.

Next, consider how you could reword or modify each statement to more closely match the abilities and credentials listed in the job description. This raises your chances of advancing in your application and even receiving a job offer by enabling you to customize your resume for the particular role.

Pay more attention to tasks and accomplishments than job titles
You may believe your career history and the titles you've held determine whether or not you get employed. When emphasizing relevant experience on your CV, the duties and accomplishments listed under each of these job titles matter far more. As an illustration, let's say you recently graduated from college and have limited work experience in the marketing sector. You've only worked as a camp counselor, but you'd like to pursue a career as a marketing coordinator.

You can use examples like "Speaking with parents to market different programs and persuade them to enroll their child in more than one program" or "Successfully sold additional programs to increase child enrollment by 15%" to illustrate how your work as a camp counselor translates to a role as a marketing coordinator.

Update your professional background and skill set to match the requirements of the job description.
Use your professional experience, education, and skills to your benefit by highlighting the pertinent experiences you've gained over your career, rather than excluding any of them. Maintain job titles unchanged, but try to reword duties or achievements to better align them with the job description. Additionally, go over the required applicant talents and list the ones that accurately represent your technical and people skills.

Embedding keywords and phrases from the job description into your CV is crucial because a lot of firms use applicant tracking systems that flag applications that contain pertinent keywords.

USING KEYWORDS
Specific competencies, expertise, skills, and qualities that hiring managers and recruiters want in a candidate are reflected in resume keywords and phrases. Job-related nouns that highlight your qualifications for a position as well as your hard and soft abilities make up your keywords. Action verbs highlight your accomplishments from previous encounters. Employers or systems look for phrases that combine keywords and action verbs.

Why are key phrases and keywords on resumes important? Because most organizations utilize Applicant Tracking Systems (ATS) to electronically pre-scan applications, screening precisely for job-related keywords and phrases, keywords and phrases plays a significant role.

The complex ATS software can be configured to:

Look for resumes using terms associated with the job specifications.

Rank and count resumes according to the frequency of keywords.

Give additional significance to certain terms.
Identify keyword stuffing

Give a resume more weight if it includes a keyword in a phrase together with other relevant skills.

Because of the sophistication of this technology, it's critical to choose keywords and phrases wisely. Recruiters will just need a few seconds to review a resume manually to find the action verbs and desired nouns.

Advice on locating keywords and phrases for resumes
To determine the ideal terms and phrases to include on your application, use the following advice:

Check job postings for the talents the business is looking for.

Examine job postings for identical positions.
Check out the business's webpage.

Examine the qualifications and background of positions at a higher level.

Look for skills the employer is looking for in job postings. Your first step in choosing the terms and phrases you wish to include on your cover letter and resume is to read through the job posting. Companies will specify exactly what they look for in an extraordinary candidate, and they frequently include the most sought-after abilities in the opening line of their job posting. Make sure you underline any keyword you come across in the job description as you read it.

Examine job postings for the same position.
Examining multiple job ads for the same post can also help you determine which keywords and phrases to include in your resume for a certain job title. Once you have looked over ten more job advertising, determine which keywords and phrases are most frequently utilized. These are perhaps the most sought-after for the job for which you are seeking. To quickly determine the most popular keywords, simply copy and paste the text of the advertisement into a word cloud generator.

Look at the business's webpage.
Searching the company's website will yield additional keywords that are consistent with its mission and vision. If these terms align with your values, using them will demonstrate your suitability for the organization.

Examine the qualifications and background of positions at higher levels.

Examining a few job postings for positions that are a step above the one you want is a terrific method to get keywords and phrases for your cover letter and CV. In the same way that you would when examining employment advertisements for your role, evaluate the wording. This time, to differentiate yourself from other applicants who might not have those superior skill sets and expertise, you should include in your application any common skills that are mentioned throughout the job adverts for the higher-level post.

If appropriate, list a few advanced talents you'd like to pick up in your resume's "areas of interest" section. Hiring supervisors will see that you are motivated and driven to learn such abilities.

How to incorporate phrases and keywords into your cover letter and resume

To properly list keywords and phrases in your application, adhere to the following fundamental guidelines:

Use variations of keywords.
Put location-based keywords in your content.
For most of your keywords and phrases, use hard skills.
Put essential terms and phrases all across your resume.

Make use of keyword variants
Employ a variety of acronyms and synonyms for your keywords to cover any variations that an employer would look for. Employing a broad range of words and phrases can highlight your varied skills and improve the likelihood that a resume scanner will select yours from a sizable application pool. Generally speaking, the ATS won't look for abbreviations until a recruiter enters in a specific one. Thus, when mentioning your "B.A.", it's also a good idea

to add "Bachelor of Arts." Make use of as many relevant keywords and phrases as you can for the assignment.

Use keywords that are location-based.
Because of your proximity to the job, the applicant tracking system (ATS) or human reader will find you more easily if you include your city and state on your resume. Recruiters consider location a major consideration for filling non-remote roles. Your address should be at the top of your resume, but you should also mention your city and state in the resume introduction, along with the job title. This makes it simple for readers and scanners to identify those two crucial terms.

For the majority of your keywords and phrases, use hard skills.
Even so, it's crucial to include soft skills in your cover letter and CV so that potential employers can get a general sense of your personality and the qualities you can offer their business. However, phone and in-person interviews are superior for evaluating soft skills, so take your time describing your technical expertise, education, and work history. Hard skills are typically given priority by ATS filters since they are easier to measure.

Use relevant keywords and phrases all across your CV.
These terms should be used in your resume in four key locations. They are as follows:

In the First Paragph of your CV
Regardless of how you choose to start your resume and highlight your most important qualifications, you should

use the most pertinent terms and expressions to demonstrate your value to an employer. Additionally, the opening section of your resume includes keywords in context, which both human and ATS readers may readily identify. It's crucial to remember that the employer's job title and the firm name should be the top two keywords on any resume in this area.

Another great location to contextualize keywords is in your job history section, where you can link them to extra experiences and talents. Here's where you would take an action verb like "managed software development projects" and mix it with a keyword noun.

In the section on Skills

You should list not just your strongest competencies but also any hardware and software you have used in the past in your skills section. To keep the ATS reading your resume, limit the number of terms you use to the most common ones. For even more clarity, you might choose to categorize your skills.

In the section on Education and trainings

Employers occasionally run background checks on candidates who have a particular educational background, like Ivy League training. But, the majority of the time, they are searching for a specific degree, which might be taken into account right away when deciding whether to advance a candidate through the recruiting process.

SEVEN RESUME-TAILORING TIPS

It is possible to write a customized resume job description that attracts recruiters and passes the applicant tracking system. Here's how to go about it:

Make use of the top half of the first page of your resume.

One of the first things recruiters and hiring managers see on your CV is your job description, along with your contact details and resume summary.

Your job description section should be in the top part of your resume because recruiters only have around seven seconds to decide whether to move on to the next round or rule you out.

Examine the position's unique job listing.

Examine the job posting line by line and consider the following questions:

Does the job description part of my CV expressly say that I am capable of performing the duties of this position?

"Am I speaking in the same way as it says in the job listing?"

"Have I highlighted any accomplishments or experiences that are directly related to the primary duties or requirements listed in the job posting?"

This can help you identify any skills and keywords that are missing from your resume and make it less generic.

Give details

You must provide the recruiting manager with a detailed account of your past and present employment. Being precise is the greatest approach to take in this.

Include the name and address of the company, your official job title, and the length of time you worked there at the beginning of each resume job description.

Align the job listing's keywords and capabilities

The simplest method to show that you're a better fit than the competition is to use phrasing, keywords, and buzzwords that are similar to those in the job ad.

Take words from the job posting and carefully insert them into your job description and other resume sections to make sure the ATS can find your resume.

However, take care not to overuse keywords on your CV.

Write your job title.

It is common for recruiters to look for candidates with prior experience, so be sure to include your work titles explicitly.

If the position is new to you, include a statement about it in the summary of your resume. If at all feasible, use the same job title as stated in the job listing.

Include the extent of your achievements
Choose carefully what you include. Give successes more weight than obligations at work.

Your job and responsibilities should be described using action verbs and numbers. The numbers demonstrate how well you performed. Using action verbs in your resume makes it easier to read and more engaging.

Never tell lies
Reducing or enhancing the importance of your resume's talents is not the same as lying on it (which we most strongly advise against).

Few candidates possess all the necessary abilities and credentials. Making sure hiring managers see the ones you do have is the goal of customizing your resume.

CHAPTER 4

QUANTIFYING ACHIEVEMENTS AND IMPACT

Quantifying your accomplishments on your CV is one of the best methods to demonstrate to potential employers how important and useful you are. Here's how to evaluate your accomplishments:

Make use of numbers and percentages:
When you describe your achievements, use exact numbers and percentages. A better phrase would be, for example, "Increased sales by 20% in Q2" rather than "Sales improved."

Highlight Achievements through Metrics:
Ascertain which performance metrics are most crucial for your industry and role. Utilize these metrics to draw attention to your accomplishments.

Put Outcomes First:
Stress outcomes and results, such as earnings, savings on expenses, or productivity increases.

Use Action Verbs
In each bullet point, the strongest action verbs that demonstrate how you will help the team achieve the goals should be used first. To give an example, consider the statement, "Started a marketing campaign that increased website traffic by 15%."

Context Is Vital
Provide background information to readers so they can understand the importance of your achievements. "Managed a team of 10 and achieved a 98% customer satisfaction rate," as an instance.

Highlight Your Achievements That Are Relevant to the Position:
Tailor your measurable achievements to the specific role that you are applying for. Focus on accomplishments that meet the requirements of the position.

Use Consistent Formatting:
Continue measuring your successes throughout your CV using the same methodology. Use bullets and bold text to make them stand out.

Avoid using jargon:
Ensure that your quantifiable accomplishments are easy to understand and relatable to a broad audience. Don't use industrial jargon.

Be accurate and truthful:
Only exact and substantiated quantitative successes ought to be mentioned. Lying about your accomplishments can come up during interviews or at employment.

List a variety of your successes, including those related to projects, collaboration, leadership, and individual contributions. This provides you with a clear image of your capabilities.

Quarterly sales revenue increased by 25% as a consequence of strategic pricing adjustments and focused marketing initiatives.

Project turnaround time was shortened by thirty percent through the implementation of process improvements and the streamlining of workflow procedures.

received a 95% customer satisfaction rating by providing exceptional customer service and answering client concerns and questions right away.

Including quantitative examples of your successes and influence on your resume will help you stand out from the competition and effectively show prospective employers how valuable you are.

THE POWER OF NUMBERS IN RESUMES

Making a CV that stands out and effectively communicates your skills, experience, and worth to potential employers is crucial in the competitive job market of today. While it's important to communicate your qualifications understandably and succinctly, one effective strategy that can help your resume stand out is the use of measurable facts. By including facts, figures, and quantitative successes in your professional biography, you can strengthen its credibility, present a clearer picture of the value you bring to a firm, market your experience more successfully, and create a more engaging narrative about your career. In this post, we'll examine the key factors, trade-offs, challenges, and overall outcomes of using statistics to quantify your CV.

Verifying Your Experience: When reviewing resumes, recruiters and hiring managers want evidence of your accomplishments and the influence you made in previous positions. Numbers may back up your claims and provide verifiable proof of your skills. As an illustration, you could put it in the following quantitative form: "boosted sales by 30% within six months," rather than merely "increased sales." By providing exact figures, you demonstrate your ability to generate results and give potential employers a benchmark by which to assess your skills.

Giving a Clearer Picture of Your Reward: Companies give rewards to candidates who can succinctly and clearly articulate their value to the organization. You can use numbers to illustrate the extent of your work. Saying "devised and executed strategic marketing campaigns that generated a 20% increase in customer engagement and a

15% rise in revenue," for example, would be a better sentence to use than simply "developed marketing campaigns." Quantifying your achievements can help you convey the impact you can have in your next career.

Adding Numbers to Your Experience to Improve It: Your CV will be more marketable and validate your experience if it has figures. Recruiters are more likely to pay attention to quantifiable information than to nonspecific remarks on applications, which they often scan. You can feel accomplished and differentiate yourself from other candidates for the same job with the help of numbers. Finding a balance and avoiding overcrowding the CV with content, however, is imperative. Focus on highlighting the most notable achievements to ensure that the information is legible and clear.

Enhancing Your Narrative: Your CV is a narrative tool that should entice companies to extend an invitation to speak with you. You can convey a more engaging story about your career trajectory by including data in your story. Employers can see your achievements and see how you may benefit their company by using numbers, which also add context and validate your qualifications. To highlight your talents and match them to the particular criteria of the position you're pursuing, use statistics strategically.

Trade-offs and Challenges: Quantifying your CV has its benefits, but you should be aware of the trade-offs and difficulties that come with it. Finding trustworthy and accurate data to back up your accomplishments is one challenge. Make sure the figures you provide can be independently verified and will hold up in an interview or when references are checked. Furthermore, not every accomplishment is immediately quantifiable. Qualitative descriptions, as opposed to numerical representations alone, maybe a more effective way to communicate soft abilities like cooperation and leadership. A well-rounded résumé must strike a balance between qualitative strengths and measurable accomplishments.

Examining the Effect: Give much thought to how numbers will affect the reader of your resume before including them. Use statistics in a way that is relevant to the sector and the particular position you are applying for. Certain industries—like finance or sales, for example— may place a greater emphasis on quantifiable indicators than others. To make sure that your approach reflects the values of the organization and demonstrates your aptitude for the position, research the expectations and preferences of the industry you are targeting.

Quantifying your experience on your CV with statistics can help you sell your expertise, demonstrate your value, authenticate your experience, and effectively communicate your professional story. But it's crucial to find a balance and take into account the drawbacks and trade-offs of this strategy. You can improve your chances of differentiating yourself from the competition and landing the job you want by carefully utilizing quantifiable data, adjusting it for the industry, and making sure it's accurate. Recall that the objective is to craft an engaging and well-rounded story that highlights your skills and appeals to prospective employers.

Consider asking yourself...
You can find chances to quantify your accomplishments and talents and give your CV more weight and legitimacy by asking yourself these questions and thinking back on your prior experiences.

1. How can I measure the significance of my past positions' accomplishments?

2. What precise figures or indicators, like income produced, expenses avoided, or percentage improvements, can I link to my accomplishments?

3. How have I helped the business expand or the company's bottom line, and how can I quantify my contributions?

4. Have I ever spearheaded or been a part of any projects or efforts that produced measurable results?

5. Is it possible for me to put a number on the number of teams I've led or worked with?

6. Have I won any prizes or been acknowledged for my work? If so, how many and what kind of distinctions have I received?

7. Is it possible to measure the efficiency gains I've made, like shorter turnaround times, more output, or more efficient procedures?

8. Have I met or surpassed any sales or income goals, and if so, by how much?

9. Is it possible to put a number on how many clients or customers I have brought on board, kept, or oversaw?

10. How have I helped to increase customer happiness or retention, and is it possible to measure the gains in KPIs like repeat business or customer feedback ratings?

11. Have I given team members training or mentoring, and if so, is it possible to measure their progress or the results of it?
Is it possible to measure the effectiveness of marketing campaigns or initiatives that I have led, in terms of improved website traffic, social media interaction, or lead generation?
13. How have I helped with cost-cutting initiatives, and is it possible for me to calculate the savings?

14. Is it possible to monitor the effects of any process enhancements or quality control techniques I've put in place?

15. Can I measure things like project duration, budget adherence, or customer satisfaction ratings? Have I contributed to successful project completions?

Adding numbers to your resume is a great way to quantify your accomplishments, show off your influence, build your reputation, and differentiate yourself from the competition. You can make a strong CV that highlights your value and improves your chances of getting interviews and job offers by utilizing the power of numbers.

DEMONSTRATING ACHIEVEMENTS WITH METRICS

Metrics are statistical or numerical indicators that demonstrate how successfully you accomplished a particular goal or performed in a particular area. Metrics may assist you in articulating your value proposition, showcasing your competencies, and proving that you meet the demands and expectations of the employer. Additionally, metrics might assist you in avoiding general or ambiguous remarks that do not set you apart from other contenders. For instance, you may state that you "led a team of 10 salespeople to achieve 120% of the annual quota" as opposed to "managed a team of salespeople".

How to select measurements

Your CV should have measurements that are quantifiable, precise, and pertinent. Metrics must be relevant to meet job requirements and the objectives and priorities of the company. To be specific, the measurements must be narrow and unambiguous rather than vague and wide. Measurable metrics are those that are predicated on evidence and facts rather than conjecture or opinion. You must evaluate the job description, do a background study on the business and the sector, and determine your greatest achievements and outcomes to select the appropriate metrics.

Methods for displaying metrics

Effectively presenting your metrics on your resume can influence how the company views and assesses them. To achieve this, quantify your measurements using figures, percentages, or dollar amounts, then describe them using action verbs and positive adjectives. Additionally, use bullet points to arrange your measurements so they are easy to scan. To add context and information to your metrics, such as the problem or circumstance you encountered, the action you did, and the outcome you attained, you can also utilize the PAR (Problem-Action-Result) or STAR (Situation-Task-Action-Result) frameworks. These will provide insightful metrics to back up your arguments.

Metric examples broken down by industry

Depending on your sector, career, and objectives, the metrics you include on your resume may change. On the other hand, several popular metrics apply to a wide range of domains and roles; they include measures related to revenue, sales, or profit; productivity, efficiency, or quality; metrics related to customers, clients, or stakeholders; and metrics related to teams, leadership, or management. For instance, you can report on sales volume or revenue growth in marketing; accuracy and standard compliance in accounting; test score improvement and graduation rate in education; functionality, dependability, and security in engineering; and patient satisfaction and safety procedures in healthcare. In the end, the appropriate measures will show how valuable you are to the company.

Adding to your CV

Adding resources or documents to your resume that offer more details that hiring managers or recruiters could find useful is known as adding supplemental information. This data clarifies exceptional situations or aids in creating a more complete picture of your history, training, experience, and qualifications.

You usually can't go into great detail about your experience or unique skill set on a resume because it should only highlight the most important aspects of your schooling and employment history. Including extra material with your resume ensures that hiring managers get the most comprehensive understanding of your professional background.

Why should your resume be sent with additional information?
If a hiring manager or recruiter asks for information that isn't on your resume, you should submit it with your resume. Additional documents ought to improve your reputation and showcase your strengths and expertise. For instance, you can utilize addenda to describe noteworthy trips, leadership roles, community involvement, and language proficiency.

In addition, you should think about providing further details in the following circumstances:

For an undergraduate or graduate degree, more data is needed.
You have gaps in your employment history.
You have an employment history or volunteer experience that isn't on your CV, such as an internship.
Your resume does not mention any licenses or credentials, and your education section does not list any relevant training.

You belong to professional associations, particularly if you play an active or leadership position in the community.

You work as an independent contractor and have references from clients.

You have experience giving public speeches and would like to discuss the specifics of your speaking engagements. You also want to share the contents of your published books or articles.

Improve your cover letter.
Highlight your abilities with a resume expert's assistance.
Advice on how to add extra material to your resume
The following ten suggestions will help you include more material with your resume:

Check the recipient's address.
Make sure you are submitting your resume, application for a job, and any supporting documents to the right person and via the right route. These files could need to be uploaded on the company website, uploaded to a job search website, or sent to a hiring manager or recruiter.
Notify your recruiter that you will be providing more data.
Notify the hiring manager or recruiter that you plan to send any additional papers with your CV so they know to anticipate them. Make sure the recruiter is aware of this fact so they may distribute your papers to managers or business owners together with your resume and application.

Make sure the data is pertinent.
Verify that the material you wish to include in your resume is pertinent to the job for which you are applying. Any additional resources should give a favorable, in-depth overview of what makes you stand out from the competition. If you want recruiters to look over additional documents, make sure they are relevant to your capacity to carry out the duties of the position.

For example, you may attach an additional document explaining how you managed a group of fifteen volunteers on a volunteer foreign service trip while applying for a managerial position. On the other hand, details regarding your sports accomplishments from ten years ago in high school might not be pertinent to a current position.
Review and edit for accuracy
Make sure you properly review all documents before forwarding them to a prospective employer. Make sure you have all the information required as specified in the application and check your spelling and punctuation. To ensure there are no errors, think about having a friend or relative review your CV, cover letter, and any supporting materials.

SUPPLEMENTING YOUR RESUME
Before an interview, think about using additional documents to clarify special conditions. You may want to go into detail about some personal or professional situations, like:
Medical conditions
Caregiving obligations
Major personal achievements

A retired service member, for instance, might talk about an injury sustained during their time in the military, particularly if they need specific tools or modifications to carry out their job responsibilities.

Talk about the gaps in employment.
You can go into further detail about any gaps in your work experience on a supplemental page that goes with your resume. You could want to go into depth about your decision to travel, finish a volunteer project, obtain a degree, or participate in an internship or other unpaid training opportunity. You can also talk about the professional or personal qualities you gained from these events and how they make you a more desirable candidate.

CHAPTER 5

COVER LETTER OVERVIEW

Sending a cover letter with your resume is a common practice when looking for jobs. It acts as a summary of your qualifications and a tailored statement of your interest in the job and the organization.

A cover letter serves as a brief introduction to you that highlights your best qualities and pertinent experience while succinctly expressing your interest in a position. It's critical to tailor your cover letter to each position to show that you have done your homework on the goals and values of the company.

A cover letter is a one-page document that you send with your resume to give further details about your experiences and qualifications for the position you're applying for. Usually, it consists of three or four brief paragraphs. Because it provides the recruiter with the first opportunity to review your qualifications and determine whether you are a suitable fit for the role, a cover letter is crucial. While it's not necessary for every job application, it's a good idea to attach one. In addition to demonstrating to the company your seriousness about the position, the extra effort sets you apart from other applicants in the letter.

TYPES OF COVER LETTERS
Cover letters fall into four broad categories:

1. Application cover letter
This is the most typical format for a cover letter used by job applicants. This conventional approach contains information about your work history that is pertinent to the job posting's requirements. It's also a chance to discuss information that's not on your resume, such as a job move, a hiatus in employment, or why you're thrilled to work for a certain organization.

2. Referral cover letter
When applying for a job, a referral cover letter is particularly helpful because it includes the name of the current employee who referred you to the open position. Having a referral can help you stand out from the competition when applying for jobs. To keep the person who referred you informed of your application progress, you might want to submit a copy of your resume and cover letter.

3. Letter of interest
A letter of interest is a cover letter that expresses your interest in a position at a company you would like to work for. Even if a company doesn't publish jobs publicly, it could still be seeking suitable candidates. With this kind of

cover letter, you proactively express your interest in working with the recruiting manager.

Consider getting in touch with the recruiter or hiring manager to follow up on your question a few weeks after submitting the letter of interest. You can demonstrate your passion for working for the organization while keeping the call or email brief and professional. Sending them a phone call or email might also help them remember you.

4. Value proposition letter
A value proposition letter is a synopsis that highlights your qualifications, accomplishments, and potential contribution to an organization. Typically, this kind of brief cover letter serves as a CV summary or a response to the "tell me about yourself" question in an interview.

WHAT TO INCLUDE IN YOUR COVER LETTER
Your most intriguing and pertinent experiences and qualifications for the available position can be included in your cover letter. The following information is crucial to have in your cover letter:

How do you fulfill the requirements of the work?
Describe your background and experience in-depth, emphasizing how they directly affect your chances of succeeding in the new role. Examine the job description carefully and identify particular areas that align with your areas of expertise. Provide percentages or figures to illustrate your credentials. For instance, if you're applying for a marketing job that necessitates in-depth SEO knowledge, you may explain how, throughout your two

years of employment, you trained three new marketing associates on SEO best practices and worked on multiple successful SEO initiatives in your previous role.

Why you would like a job with the company?

Employers are interested in learning why you choose to work for them. They are looking to hire someone who shows genuine interest in the responsibilities of the position and excitement for the business. Describe how you can achieve your career goals by working there. It's critical to be real. Talk about the company's development and reputation to demonstrate that you did your homework on the business and that you want to help it succeed.

Additional components of a cover letter could be:

Important anecdotes: Share a captivating anecdote about your involvement with the organization, sector, or nature of the position. For instance, you may say that you've been a patron of this business for more than ten years or that ever since reading an article in the newspaper last year, you've dreamed of working in this field.

A call to action: Something like "I look forward to hearing more about this opportunity," which is a courteous and non-binding call to action, conveys your enthusiasm, and gives potential employers a reason to get in touch with you.

PURPOSE AND IMPORTANCE OF COVER LETTERS

Depending on the position you apply for, some organizations will give a cover letter more weight than others, but it's still a valuable weapon to have in your toolbox to help you stand out. A prospective employer can see from your cover letter that you are not only qualified but also possess outstanding writing abilities. Here are several justifications for the significance of a cover letter:

It narrates your Story

Before your initial interview, use the cover letter as a chance to introduce yourself and your narrative. An employer gains more insight into your existing circumstances while you get the opportunity to demonstrate your suitability for the position and explain what makes you a good fit. For instance, you can be an entry-level worker seeking to obtain professional work experience, or you might have quit your prior employer and be attempting to start a new career path.

One of the key goals of a cover letter is to control the message about your work history, which can be beneficial. You have the chance to outline your brand and highlight the essential values you can provide to the organization in this application paper. A recruiter may have their initial impression of you and your qualifications from this letter. Think about using this chance to convince a hiring manager that you're the best candidate for the position.

It strengthens the bond with the employer.

Developing a network is essential to landing a job that fits your professional objectives. Writing a cover letter is no different. A cover letter introduces you to an employer whereas a resume just outlines your accomplishments. This is the primary distinction between sending a cover letter and a resume.

It is strongly advised that you demonstrate which professional achievements matter the most to you and why. By outlining your achievements, you're showcasing what and why you find meaning in your profession. If you're fresh to the sector or the workforce, describe how your experience and skill set will be useful in your future position. Emphasize how your education, part-time work, or volunteer experience have equipped you with transferable talents that will make you effective at their organization.

It describes how you are related to the person who recommended you.
You may have used networking to your advantage to obtain employment. Perhaps you learned about the opportunity at a networking event, participated in an informative interview, or know someone who works there (a friend or family member, for example). In any case, a cover letter describes how you got to know your referrer and why you decided to apply after speaking with them.

BUILDING A CONNECTION WITH EMPLOYERS
Putting some personality into your cover letter is a really helpful step in the job search. Numerous employers have implemented application scanning programs. These algorithms scan your resume for pertinent keywords before human eyes ever lay eyes on it. You want to establish a good rapport with the employer if they get your cover letter. You have the best chance of moving on to the interview phase with this link.

A cover letter has two objectives. First and foremost, the cover letter asks you to emphasize your special abilities, qualifications, and expertise. Second, you might express your interest in the company through your cover letter. In addition to being about you, the cover letter is also about them.

You must demonstrate to your employer that you have done your research on the company's ethos, founding narrative, and mission statement to pique their interest. Prove to them that you kept these points in mind when you wrote this introduction letter for them. Recall that every résumé that recruiters read through is trying to sell something. A unique dynamic arises when an employer perceives that you are going above and beyond the call of duty to establish a personal connection rather than just trying to close a deal.

Establishing a Relationship

You have to establish sincere connections between the company's objectives and ideals and your own. Give a brief example to illustrate your grasp of their mission statement from your career, or personal, if suitable. Citing or making reference to content from their website will demonstrate how well you have summed up their goal statement and how it fits with their corporate culture. You must establish a link when you relate this to your personal work background.

Make Yourself Unique

Create a summary of your personality by combining the aspects of your career and life experiences. It is not appropriate to list every job you have ever had on your cover letter. Make connections between the roles you have held and the experiences you have had in your cover letter.

You can demonstrate to your company how your prior experiences make you the most qualified candidate for the position in this way.

Talk about the job description.
It demonstrates your careful consideration of the role when you align your skills with particular instances from the job description. Customizing your cover letter for every business demonstrates that you are not sending in a generic application, even if you are applying for similar positions at different companies. While you don't have to start from scratch every time, a few crucial changes might greatly impact each prospective employer.

Make sure to identify any professional experiences or talents you haven't yet acquired and express them as goals you hope to achieve. This demonstrates to the recruiter your appreciation for the company's willingness to provide you with this opportunity to expand your skill set.

CHAPTER 6

STRUCTURE AND COMPONENTS OF A COVER LETTER

A well-written cover letter can significantly enhance your job application by providing a personalized introduction to potential employers. Here's a typical structure and the key components of a cover letter:

Details of Contact (Header)
Similar to resumes, cover letters are divided into sections. First things first: is a header necessary for a cover letter? Indeed.

The header of your cover letter is your first chance to establish a brand; it's more than just a list of ways people can contact you. It has to be identical to the top of your CV to present your application as a well-put-together, professional bundle.

Not only does this symmetry seem good, but it also demonstrates how carefully and methodically you approached your job application.

So what should the header of a cover letter contain?

The following are the essential components of a cover letter header:

Name
Location
Email address
LinkedIn URL (Optional)
Phone number
The date

Salutation
During your job search, initial impressions are crucial. This is the reason the salutation in a cover letter is so crucial.

This is the first opportunity to create a customized cover letter and show the firm that you are interested in getting to know them personally. When you know the hiring manager's name, it's best to speak with them directly. It presents you as a candidate who values interpersonal interaction, conveys respect, and demonstrates that you have done your research.

Is there any reason not to begin your cover letter with "To whom it may concern"?

Because a personalized greeting makes you stand out amid the throng of applications that inundate an inbox in today's employment market. It conveys to the hiring manager right away that you are focused and pay attention to details.

This small action has the power to turn a generic cover letter from a one-size-fits-all document into a customized conversation starter that appeals to the hiring manager.

How to locate the name of the hiring manager
It could seem hard to get the recruiting manager's name, but it's usually easier than you think.

Here are various methods to find this crucial piece of knowledge:

LinkedIn: Your best bet is to start with a professional network. If you're looking for a specialist position, look up the organization online and go through the personnel lists, paying particular attention to individuals with titles like "Hiring Manager," "Recruitment Officer," or department heads.

Company website: On the "Team" or "About Us" pages of the business, information is occasionally buried in plain sight. Larger businesses may display the names, job titles, and contact details of their employees.

Calling in: Sometimes the best strategy is to be straightforward. Speak with the HR or front desk staff of the business. Introduce yourself, be courteous, and state that you would like your cover letter to be addressed correctly. Most will be glad to assist.

Outreach through networking: Lean on your network. Find out from mentors or coworkers who could know the recruiting manager of the job you're interested in. Most of the time, you can get the name you need through a mutual link.

Social media Search: Businesses frequently provide information about their staff and recent hiring on websites like Instagram, Twitter, and LinkedIn. The correct name might be found with a fast search.

OPENING PARAGRAPH
Your cover letter's introductory paragraph is your opportunity to grab the reader's attention and lay out the framework for your story.

This part of your cover letter should contain a quick introduction to yourself, a summary of the job for which you are applying, and a strong argument for why the role would be a fantastic fit for your qualifications and career goals.

How to grab your reader's attention in the opening paragraph
The first paragraph of your introduction needs to do more than j introduce yourself; it needs to pique readers' interest. This is how to make sure it fulfills that:

Commence with a flourish: Start by making a powerful claim or highlighting a noteworthy success in your career. Alternatively, a succinct, audacious statement expressing your excitement for the organization may work just as well.

Don't tell, show: Provide a brief story or impactful example from your experience that highlights your skills and aligns with the company's requirements or beliefs.
Adjust your voice: Make sure your writing style aligns with the company's culture. While a typical company could value a formal and direct approach, a startup might value a more relaxed and creative introduction.

Put some style in it: Don't let your style overpower your professionalism. Make sure the combination reflects your distinct professional style.

Research findings: Mention a recent development that you found impressive about the company to demonstrate your current awareness of and genuine interest in their work.
Explain the what and the why. Express your excitement for the position and your unique value proposition in clear and concise terms.

Here is an example of a beginning paragraph for a cover letter:
"Consider a marketing approach that is so compelling that it starts a movement in addition to grabbing attention. Throughout the last ten years, as a marketing manager, I have raised brand engagement by an average of 65% annually, and that has been the cornerstone of my strategy. Inspired by [Company Name]'s recent ground-breaking campaign on sustainability—a topic I've been passionate about since I was a little child—I'm excited to apply my

skill at telling engaging stories to the position of Head of Marketing.

Why is this a compelling opening?

Storytelling is engaged: "Imagine" is used as the beginning verb, which is far more interesting than a more conventional sentence like "My name is."

Measurable accomplishments: It contains a precise, quantifiable accomplishment (raising brand engagement by 65% annually), which supports the applicant's assertions and demonstrates a history of success.

Personal connection: The applicant's interest in the company seems sincere and well-founded because of the statement of a longstanding enthusiasm for sustainability.

Alignment with company values: The mention of the business's sustainability campaign implies a natural cultural fit and shows that the applicant has done their homework and understands the company's principles.

Emphasis on contribution: The applicant immediately tackles how they can contribute to the company's success rather than just what they hope to receive from the employment by expressing a desire to bring experience in developing appealing narratives.

You'll have a better chance of drawing the reader into the body of your cover letter if you can make all of those points stand out in it.

BODY PARAGRAPHS

The main content of your cover letter is your message. This is the phase in which you initiate your career by matching your abilities and background to the requirements of the current position.

This section should have a clear and appealing structure, with one to three paragraphs that each have a specific function.

Your prior achievements and the possible future contributions you could make to the firm should be linked in the opening paragraph. The second and third paragraphs, for example, might be utilized to elaborate on your accomplishments, experiences, and pertinent talents while also demonstrating your understanding of the company's objectives and difficulties.

How to highlight Relevant Skills and Experiences

Here's how to design a cover letter body that hiring managers will find compelling:

Contextualize and Customize: Make sure every example you provide reflects the requirements of the position. It all comes down to relevancy: explain to the reader how and why your experience qualifies you for the particular position.

Quantify your impact: To give your accomplishments more weight, use measurements and figures. Numbers speak louder than words, whether the goal is to increase sales by a specific percentage or cut costs through creative solutions.

Using the problem, action, result (PAR) technique, list the difficulties you had, the steps you took, and the outcome of your work for each skill or experience you share. This approach demonstrates your way of thinking and problem-solving abilities.

Align to the mission of the business: By connecting your experience to the company's ongoing projects or objectives, you can demonstrate that you've done your homework. This exhibits ambition and forward-thinking in addition to alignment.

Storytelling with substance: Construct an interesting tale out of your experiences. Your objective is to take the reader on a journey that demonstrates development, significance, and relevance to the position.

Be succinct and explicit: Steer clear of sophisticated language and jargon. To ensure that your comments are understood clearly, the body of your cover letter should be simple to read and comprehend.

Here's an illustration of what ought to be in the body of a cover letter:

While I was employed at XYZ Corp, a leader in environmentally friendly packaging, I led a change that was initially met with strong opposition from our clientele as well as from within. Redefining ecological packaging as a smart, consumer-driven option instead of an expensive alternative was a difficult task. I planned to start an awareness campaign that emphasized both the long-term financial advantages and the environmental effects. With this project, XYZ Corp. was positioned as a thought leader in the market, and customer involvement increased by 120%.

I oversaw a cross-functional team in my most recent project to address a 15% decline in market share brought on by heightened competition. Through a comprehensive competitive study and consumer feedback loop, we were able to pinpoint the main areas in which our messaging was unsuccessful. I oversaw the creation of a customer success-driven brand revival effort that was centered on our key competencies. As a result, during the first quarter following the campaign, market share increased by 25%.

In every position, I have made sure that my activities are in line with both the company's short-term objectives and its long-term vision. For example, I launched a successful pilot program at XYZ Corp. that used machine learning to personalize client interactions, foreseeing the development of AI in marketing and resulting in a 30% increase in customer retention rates.

But keep in mind that different facts will be highlighted in each cover letter. Your cover letter should be tailored to the particular position you are applying for.

This degree of customization might seem laborious, but it's essential.

CLOSING PARAGRAPH

The closing paragraph, one of the final major sections of a formal cover letter, serves as a deliberate attempt to entice the reader to schedule an interview rather than merely providing a summary. In this section, you should restate your interest in the job, provide a brief explanation of why you're a good fit, and convey your excitement about the opportunity to help the organization.

You can also use this space to make a call to action, like saying that you would like a personal interview to go over your application in greater detail.

How to conclude your cover letter.

Reiterate your Value: Briefly reiterate how your experiences and talents fit the position and can help the business.

Individual touch: Demonstrate your sincere excitement and self-assurance in your capacity to fill the position. Allow them to sense your excitement and willingness to accept the challenges it brings.

Call to Action: Motivate the hiring manager to move forward. You may mention you're excited to talk about how you can benefit their team or that you'd be happy to share further information about how you can help them reach their objectives.

Here's an example of what your cover letter's conclusion paragraph could contain:
I'm thrilled to support [Company Name]'s creative marketing initiatives. My skill set perfectly complements

the goals of the Head of Marketing role. I'm excited to use my knowledge of digital engagement and strategic planning to create campaigns that are in line with your brand's mission. I also look forward to talking with you about how my thoughts and experience may help your business succeed. I appreciate you taking the time to review my application, and I look forward to our in-person meeting to talk about collaboration.

The Sign-off

A polished conclusion establishes the impression that your cover letter will make. It should exude formality and respect, much like the last handshake of a productive meeting.

Here's how to make sure your application is strengthened by your sign-off:

Select the appropriate conclusion: "Sincerely," "Best regards," and "Kind regards" are appropriate, polished choices. "Best" or "Warm regards" might work well if there is a more relaxed corporate culture.

Put your entire name here: To maintain formality and clarity, you should always sign off with your entire name. If you have a personal rapport with the recruiting manager, it can be meaningful to include a handwritten signature above your typed name.

Professioal Contact Information: To make follow-up easier, put your professional contact information—phone

number, email address, and LinkedIn profile URL—
beneath your name.

CHAPTER 7

WRITING A PERSUASIVE COVER LETTER

TIPS FOR COMPOSING COVER LETTERS
These pointers will assist you in crafting a cover letter that will grab the attention of an employer.

Select a suitable tone and voice. Write in your voice, but do some research on the business to get the appropriate tone and voice. For instance, a marketing design company's voice and tone might be different from that of a legal consulting organization.

Adhere to a standard format. Your cover letter can be easier to read if it follows a straightforward format. If you use a sans-serif typeface and neutral colors like black, you can prevent the reader from being distracted.

Examine the job description. Read the job description carefully before drafting a cover letter to learn what the business is looking for in an applicant. Select keywords for your cover letter that highlight the abilities and experience you have that will help them.

Observe the directions. Certain employers give candidates instructions on how to respond to queries or what details to include in their cover letter. Make sure you thoroughly read these notes.

Make sure to correctly address your contact. Occasionally, the name of the recruiting manager is unavailable. In these situations, start the letter with the name of the organization and address it to the "Dear Hiring Manager."

Vary the words you use. Try using more imaginative word choices, such as "tenacious" in place of "determined," and start your paragraph with a catchy phrase.

Don't write too much. Your cover letter's length may ultimately rely on how much information you offer and whether the employer has a minimum or maximum length requirement. To demonstrate your qualifications, be as specific and brief as you can. Keep in mind that your cover letter should be seen as a more intimate summary of your abilities rather than a resume synopsis.

The "why you?" question, or why a hiring manager should take the time to learn more about you and the potential contributions you could make to the company and position, is addressed in a cover letter. A cover letter is a condensed version of an elevator pitch that is results-driven rather than flowery.

WHEN TO SUBMIT A COVER LETTER

The following typical situations call for sending a cover letter together with your resume:

If one is needed for the position: If an employer requires a cover letter, it might say so right on the job application. Even if it states that it's optional, you could still want to write a cover letter and submit it with your application to give a more thorough explanation of why you're the best fit for the position.

If the hiring manager needs to see one during the interview process: If you apply for a job without one and are invited for an interview, the company can still require one. Although unlikely, this is still a possibility. Even in situations when a cover letter is not required, it is always a good idea to have one ready.

If you are aware of the recruiting manager's name: If you are aware of the hiring manager's name, address your cover letter to them directly. An indirect recommendation may be able to provide you with the name of a hiring manager so you may make the appropriate introduction.

If you were referred to the position, send your cover letter to the company's acquaintance. They can forward it to their organization's hiring manager or the human resources department recruiter.

SHOWCASING YOUR PERSONALITY

This is how to create a distinctive cover letter that is both professional and approachable without being unduly formal.

Grab their Attention

The recruiting manager will quickly get very sleep-deprived if your cover letter starts with an impersonal "To whom it may concern." The first step to writing a personable cover letter is to make the effort to find out the name of the person if you want the job. It's time to start your letter with a catchy introduction once you've decided who to write it to.

You're not alone if you've ever opened a cover letter with the words, "My name is _____, and I am applying for the _____ position at _____ company." The problem is, that won't make your application stand out from the countless others that are presently tucked away in a folder on the computer of your future employer. Instead, try starting your cover letter with a (relevant) anecdote about yourself or a past event that is related to the business or job.

Until you make it, pretend.

Writing a cover letter might be difficult because you are attempting to sell yourself to someone who does not know you well. This may result in a boring, extremely professional cover letter that says nothing about you and is jam-packed with job titles, talents, and clichés like "I'm a hard worker who goes above and beyond."

What happens if you act as though the hiring manager already knows how wonderful you are, that you deserve the position, and that you are the ideal candidate? The hiring manager is so sure of your excellence that all they want to know is more about you! What objectives do you have? What motivated you to apply? What qualities of your personality make you a wonderful match? What fresh concepts are you able to offer?

With this kind of thinking, you can go past the tedious process of enumerating all of your abilities and focus on what makes you unique.

Align the Voice and Tone
Your cover letter should always be written in a courteous but conversational (i.e., human) tone. The tone and voice of your cover letter must align with the firm or industry you are applying to. For instance, your cover letter for a job at a corporate bank would probably need to have a more formal tone than one for a trendy startup.

You can certainly utilize anecdotes and examples from your own life to demonstrate your personality in both, but you might want to reserve your clever anecdotes or original ideas for businesses that have a similar humorous tone in their communications or on their website.

Demonstrate Your Cultural Fit
Examining a company's website, blog, social media posts, and even job descriptions can reveal a lot about its culture. This type of material can help you learn a lot about the company's beliefs, practices, and group interests in addition to demonstrating how you fit in with the culture.

Has anyone mentioned the popular virtual staff trivia nights in a recent post? Write a brief note in your cover letter about your passion for trivia! Are yearly in-person retreats essential to the mission and culture of the organization? Tell the recruiting manager how important you find it to have annual team meetings. Is the company's culture based on the idea of remote work? Describe your background in remote work and your commitment to it. You may help the firm understand who you are by showcasing these facets of your personality in your cover letter.

Provide Personal Examples
Yes, your CV includes an overview of your qualifications and a clear, succinct rundown of all of your prior positions and skill sets. However, this does not mean that your cover letter has to be a recitation of every detail in paragraph form. Without question, the things that will make you eligible for a job are your talents and experience. However, demonstrating in your cover letter how you've applied those abilities could be the difference between being added to the "maybe" pile and getting an interview.

Remain upbeat and competent.
Avoid saying anything in your cover letter that could come across as critical or sarcastic, no matter how tempting it may be to adopt an apologetic or sardonic tone to stand out.

Sarcasm is a pleasant personality trait that you can enjoy with your friends and family, but it doesn't translate well in writing and can turn off hiring managers who aren't into your humor or don't get it yet. When sharing personal tales and stories, make sure they are positive and avoid drawing any conclusions about the firm or the reader.

Above all, maintain a professional tone throughout your cover letter. Make sure it is well-written and devoid of errors, and steer clear of frequent cover letter errors at all times.

Samples of Cover Letter Tone (Before and After)

We are aware that turning a "how-to" into a "done that" is not always simple. Here's an example of a conventional, impersonal cover letter and how to change it to make it something personal, distinctive, and captivating that will land you the interview.

To Whom It May Concern, Hiring Manager

I believe you will agree that I am the ideal candidate for the Accounting Administrator position that you posted on LinkedIn.

I am a seasoned administrative worker who is taking accounting classes at State University to broaden my understanding of the subject. I have been a high-level administrative support provider over the past seven years in a range of businesses, including finance and accounting. I'm now searching for a job that will allow me to put my administrative skills to work and offer me more chances to grow both personally and professionally.

I am a meticulous multitasker with great communication abilities, a knack for setting priorities, and the ability to oversee challenging assignments.

For further information about my background and credentials, kindly refer to the resume I've included. I appreciate your time and am looking forward to our meeting so we can talk about what I can do to help your company.

Warm regards,

Greg

Assume the position of a hiring manager. Does the cover letter above pique your interest and explain why "Jamie" is a good fit for the position? Is the tone of the cover letter interesting and personable? Regretfully, no. This is probably the most generic cover letter you have ever read, hence it will be rejected.

Greg's excitement for the firm and the role, her track record of delivering results in the real world, and her qualifications are all much better shown in the following cover letter.

Greetings, Ms. Precious

I enthusiastically submit my application to ABC Foundation for the Accounting Administrator post. With more than seven years of experience as an administrative professional, I'm sure that my background and abilities will help the accounting staff at ABC Foundation.

I have developed my career in small businesses, as you can see from my résumé attached, working in a range of administrative, bookkeeping, account representative, and client relations coordinator positions in addition to the administrative coordinator. I enjoy taking on multiple hats, and I function best in a setting where I can tackle a variety of activities.

Apart from being adaptable and quick to respond, I also have an obsession with details, especially when it comes to writing reports. In one of my most recent assignments, I had to oversee the creation of a 50-page financial report for an RFP. This required me to gather data, edit and format spreadsheets, and ensure that the final result complied with specifications. (The outcome: a $750,000 grant awarded for two years.) I put the same amount of care and attention to detail into everything I do, even the more mundane things like creating agendas for important meetings and maintaining the office's efficiency.

Not to add, I have always loved the ABC Foundation and have been a lifelong supporter of your "Feeding the Community" initiative. Having been involved from the beginning, I am delighted to see this movement grow. I've already perused your website's campaign goals for the next year, and I'm impressed with your continued outreach and expansion strategies!

I am thrilled about the possibility of collaborating with your business and would appreciate the opportunity to meet with you to discuss the advantages I can provide ABC Foundation. I truly value your consideration, and I look forward to hearing from you!

Sincerely,

Greg

Now take a moment to reflect on how you feel about this cover letter. In contrast to just another nameless job applicant with a boilerplate cover letter, Greg truly seems like the ideal candidate and a fantastic cultural match. You may have been ready to hire her before the interview!

The Ideal Balance of Tone, Personality, and Professionalism

Most businesses don't look for brainless employees who follow instructions and perform tasks in the same manner as everyone else. Selecting the right tone for your cover letter is essential because the ideal applicant will be someone who fits the company's culture and adds personality.

Cover letters are essential to the application process for many jobs since they give the hiring manager a summary of your qualifications. Making a professional, customized cover letter that emphasizes your uniqueness gives you and the company the best of both worlds!

EXPRESSING ENTHUSIASM

Even while you may think that cover letters are no longer necessary, the truth is that some hiring managers still look through them, and the information you submit matters to them. In light of this, it is important to carefully consider the message you want to deliver.

And certainly, simply saying, "Hire me," is insufficient. Everyone's application may be summed up in just two words. The best examples are usually supported with a "because" clause that explains why you should hire them.

"Hire me, because I have a ton of relevant experience," or "Hire me, because you're a two-person company and I know how to wear a ton of hats as things evolve," or the tried-and-true "Hire me, because I'm incredibly excited about this position," would be a great way to sum up your entire letter. I hope this is useful.

As you may have seen, that last line isn't quite as impactful as the first two, at least not immediately. It clarifies your curiosity, but it makes no mention of the skills you would bring to the job. It only talks about how excited you are about the work. You're ecstatic about the position, infatuated with the company, and absorbed in the industry. Nevertheless, you end up getting lost in a sea of letters that seem more like fan mail, despite your wish to stand out as someone who would go above and beyond out of genuine concern.

Please remember that a strong selling point is enthusiasm. It needs to be packaged appropriately, though, to show why employing you would be a good fit. Three of the poorest and most well-known lines can be rewritten as follows:

The Old Approach: "I've Been Dreaming for Years of Working at [Organization]"

The New Approach "I Noticed the Company Has Recently Shifted Toward [X]."

Saying that you've always wanted a job isn't relevant. First of all, anyone can make that claim. Secondly, you can't prepare a feast if you don't spend any time in the kitchen, no matter how much you've always wanted to be a great chef.

It certainly helps to have followed a company when its website was still in development. You are knowledgeable about the company's development and the target market. Because of these two factors, you would be a more valuable hire than someone who just happened to stumble onto the organization.

Focus on how your past expertise with the organization will facilitate your integration and enable you to begin working immediately. If you point out that the company seems to have altered its marketing, packaging, or anything else that only an employee or true lover of the product would know, you'll immediately demonstrate that you might offer a knowledgeable viewpoint.

The Old Approach, "I Want This Job More Than You Can Believe"

New Approach: "I Was Happy to See That [X] Is Among the Principal Duties"

Many people worry that their cover letters may seem too official and artificial. As a result, they overreach, creating the illusion that they are having a face-to-face conversation with the hiring manager about how much they would genuinely love the position. This doesn't reveal anything special about you and could be found in any cover letter; you never want your note to sound like a speech from The Bachelor to someone who can just replace "job" with "relationship."

Instead of expressing your preference for a particular position, highlight a section of the job description where you shine. One way to do this is to ask yourself follow-up questions, like "Why do you want this job so much?" Which part of it most interests you? What distinguishes you from other applicants for that role as being more qualified for that responsibility?

Instead of just conveying your general enthusiasm, use the reply to get into why you're enthusiastic and what you could offer to the table. This will make your letter much more memorable.

"I'm the biggest fan of [your company]/[your CEO]/[industry]" is a line from the past.

New Approach: "I know that X, as a devoted follower of [Industry]/[Your Company]/[Your CEO], is true."
You indeed follow the company and its creator on social media, along with every prominent industry influencer. You get alerts whenever there is news about the company and you talk about it so often that people wonder whether you work there.

You also want the interviewer to realize that you already represent their position as an ambassador and that you would be competent. However, you never want to come across as an admirer. That will also convey the idea that you are a "yes man" or "yes woman" who is happy to go to work every day and follow plans without questioning them, even if there are better solutions available.

Highlight all of the advantages of your thorough analysis of the company or sector. Are there any impending changes that you might be able to help with knowing about? Would you like to assist with any current developments or restructurings? Giving a concrete example of how you would blend in shows that you are both a fit and enthusiastic about the situation.

You're wasting precious real space when you write in depth about how much you want to work somewhere. If you take the time to tailor your cover letter and highlight your qualifications for the job, your eagerness will come across more readily and convincingly.

ALIGNING WITH COMPANY VALUES
Here are some tips on demonstrating to demonstrate your commitment to the firm's objectives and values in your cover letter.

Research the company
Before you begin writing your cover letter, do some research on the company you are applying to. Look at their website, social media pages, press releases, annual reports, and any other informational materials that can help you

comprehend their goals, principles, and achievements. Think about connecting their main concepts, pivotal words, and guiding principles to your own.

Tailor the communication

Avoid making generic or confusing statements that might apply to any function or organization. Instead, tailor your letter to the specific company and job that you are looking for. Show how your experience, education, and hobbies fit the requirements and expectations of the role. Give instances and stories from your previous and current positions, projects, or activities that demonstrate how you have developed or used the company's values. For example, if the company is creative, you could discuss how you initiated or contributed to the creation of a novel process, item, or service in your sector.

Display Enthusiasm

One of the best ways to show that you are committed to a company's goals and values is to express your enthusiasm and love for its job and working techniques. Explain why you would like to work for them, as well as the parts of their impact, offerings, and products that you find appealing. Use positive, uplifting language to convey your eagerness to become a member of their team and support their success. Rather than seeming gullible or arrogant, focus on how you can help them and be of service.

Show sincerity.

Finally, be honest and truthful in your cover letter. Never exaggerate or lie about your skills, accomplishments, or moral convictions. Never copy and paste text from templates or other websites. Do not attempt to impersonate someone you are not. Instead, use your voice and style to communicate your personality, abilities, and goals. Show why you are a good fit for the role and the company, but also emphasize your unique qualities and what you can provide that others might not. Remember to bring some personality and flair in while still being courteous, professional, and respectful.

AVOIDING COMMON PITFALLS
Here are 15 things you should never put in a cover letter, along with suggestions on what to put in its stead:

Disregarding the instructions
You must follow any policies your employer may provide. Employers usually offer comprehensive instructions on how to submit your cover letter and what information to include in it. The hiring manager should have no trouble locating the information in your cover letter that they require. Use this as an opportunity to show them that you can understand important details and follow instructions.

What to do: Go over the job description thoroughly and look for any specific instructions the company may have regarding a cover letter. Make sure you follow the instructions for sending in your cover letter and include any material that is expressly needed in the job advertisement. For example, if the job description specifies that you should save your file as a PDF, then follow that recommendation. If the guidelines ask you to address any specific questions, make sure your letter does so in an effective manner.

Using the wrong format

If you use the right format for your cover letter, the hiring manager will find it easy to read. Avoid being too creative or wordy in your cover letter, even though you still want it to stand out. You can make your message easier for people to understand by breaking up long text passages into short, concise paragraphs that highlight the most important information. Cutting back on color and graphics will assist in focusing readers' attention on your main points.

What to do: Start with a cover letter template to ensure you adhere to the proper format. Next, make any necessary changes to the template to give your letter a unique look that will help you stand out from the competitors. Your cover letter should have one-inch margins on all sides and a space between sections no longer than one page. Select a typeface that is readable at a readable size and appears professional.

State the reasons behind your job search

An explanation of your job search does not need to be included in your cover letter. This is especially important if you are looking for a new job because of a strained relationship or terrible experience from your current one.

What to do: Consider carefully what you can bring to the table if you are hired, as well as the reasons behind your interest in the role and company you are applying to. Your resume should be everything about you and your career aspirations. Only discuss your past when it is necessary to elucidate your skills, prowess, talents, and accomplishments.

Using the Same cover letter for every Job Application
Your cover letter's content must be unique and pertinent to the reader, even if you used a template to ensure that the format was correct. Crafting an exceptional cover letter necessitates customizing its content to the particular demands and specifications of the role and organization you are eyeing. It should be necessary to make changes to your cover letter each time you wish to submit it for a job.

How to start: Use the recruiting manager's name at the beginning of your letter. Make sure to provide the exact title of the position you're applying for in your cover letter. Talk about how your abilities and qualities benefit the organization and how your principles fit in with its goals, mission, and culture.

Composing without Making Research about the Orgination and the Role you are applying for.
Research is necessary before writing a cover letter that is suited to the position and the business. You may decide what information to include and what matters most to the company by doing some research on them. When composing a cover letter that engages the hiring manager and demonstrates your suitability for their organization, thorough research is frequently the most crucial component.

What to do: Go over the job description and take note of any details the firm feels are pertinent to the particular role or themselves. Next, study the purpose and vision statements of the organization and browse its website to learn more about its background, objectives, and culture.

Lastly, to obtain more information, consult external sources such as news sites, job forums, and corporate reviews.

Talking about a lack of experience or irrelevant work experience

Attempting to use your cover letter as an excuse for lacking relevant experience is another typical mistake. Even while you might want to allay the hiring manager's worries over your experience—or lack thereof—you don't want to come across as insignificant.

What to do: Pay close attention to how your past experiences have made you the most qualified applicant for the job. Talk about the lessons you've learned from your experience and how they applied to the job you're looking for. Make sure you include an explanation of how you intend to apply the abilities and information you gained from the experience to succeed in your new position and contribute value to the organization.

Neglecting to emphasize your best or most applicable Skills

Additionally, you might want to utilize your cover letter to justify to the company why specific talents that they included in the job description aren't on your CV. Just like with unrelated experience, you don't want to draw attention to a flaw or lack of ability. It is crucial to ensure that the abilities that best represent your strengths and are most pertinent to the position you are applying for are highlighted in your cover letter.

What to do: Look over the job description and identify the competencies that best align with your strongest suit. Next, consider your experiences and successes that you may utilize to demonstrate that these abilities are a strength of yours. Even if you have abilities that are relevant and can help you succeed in the work, don't mention them.

Putting Job responsibilities ahead of achievements
The responsibilities and obligations you held in each of your prior roles should be listed on your resume. You should elaborate on those responsibilities in your cover letter by talking about your professional accomplishments or how you exceeded the requirements of your position.

What to do: Discuss any honors or unique accolades you have received for your professional accomplishments. If you have accomplished several professional goals in your career, pick the most noteworthy and pertinent ones for the job you are applying for.

Salary Expectation
Unless the company expressly requests it, you should not include your present or future wage expectations in your cover letter. If you discuss compensation expectations too soon, you may be more focused on the perks of the position than on how you might help the organization.

What to do: Highlight your value to the firm and the position in your cover letter. If you are asked to provide pay expectations by the company, choose a broad range that you would feel happy with rather than a precise amount.

Failure to support Claims with Evidence

Any claims you make about your abilities, accomplishments, and skills should be backed up with information and statistics. By doing this, you can substantiate your assertions and demonstrate to the hiring manager why you are a desirable candidate.

What to do: Whenever possible, bolster assertions with facts, figures, and statistics. For instance, "helped my company save more than $5,000 per year and increased office productivity 10% by transitioning to an electronic filing system" is more definitive than "helped my company save money and increased office productivity with an electronic filing system." A resume that reads, "consistently achieved a 98% or higher quality assurance rating" conveys to the hiring manager your value as a candidate and your dedication to excellence.

Not using keywords to optimize your cover letter

Another crucial method for enhancing the effect of your cover letter is the use of keywords. To identify eligible applicants for the hiring manager's consideration, applicant tracking systems search through application materials, including cover letters. The hiring manager will also find your cover letter more memorable if it contains keywords and phrases related to the job and business.

What to do: Find the most pertinent keywords for your cover letter by reading the job description and doing some research on the business and the sector. Then, to make assertions about your value stand out, link those keywords to descriptions of your accomplishments, abilities, and capabilities.

Repeating Informartion Contained in your Resume

Your cover letter's content ought to bolster and supplement the details on your resume. It is crucial to ensure that, without going against what your CV says, your cover letter gives the hiring manager information that they cannot discover in your resume.

What to do: Use your cover letter to elaborate on facts in your resume, making the information both complementary and distinct from each other. Use your cover letter, for instance, to talk about a particular accomplishment that demonstrates some of the abilities you listed on your CV.

Using wrong tone or style

You must carefully balance formality and flexibility in your cover letter to ensure that it has the appropriate tone and style. It should be both formal enough to maintain professionalism and casual enough to demonstrate that the information is unique. A too-official tone could bore the reader, but an excessively informal tone could give the impression that you aren't serious about the application process.

What to do: Fit the company's tone and style with the information you have learned about it. Use the reader's name to personalize the letter rather than opening it with "To Whom It May Concern" or "Dear Hiring Manager." Steer clear of colloquial or vulgar language, superfluous jargon, and slang to maintain a professional tone.

Not providing a compelling call to action in your conclusion

Selling yourself to the recruiting manager in your cover letter is its main goal. Your closing should ask the hiring manager to take some action; the specifics about your qualifications and skills are your sales pitch.

What to do: Compose a concluding paragraph that urges or requests the hiring manager to take a particular action. A message like "I look forward to meeting you for an interview and working together to create a new training program" indicates to the hiring manager that you are prepared to assist the organization in reaching its objectives and that you anticipate being contacted for an interview.

Not proofreading your cover letter before sending it

A crucial step in any writing process is proofreading. If you don't take the time to proofread your cover letter before submitting it, you may overlook little issues like misspelled words, incorrect punctuation, erroneous information, and missing facts.

What to do: You can better understand the message you are expressing and how the hiring manager will interpret it by reading your cover letter aloud. As you go through the letter, make any necessary edits. Continue doing this until you are done making adjustments. Think of getting a friend or family member to proofread it as well and provide feedback. Those who are familiar with us can occasionally point out things we might have forgotten.

ADDRESSING GAPS AND CONCERNS
You have the chance to proactively explain any possible red flags in your employment history and reassure the employer of your eligibility for the role by addressing any gaps or concerns in your cover letter. The following advice might help you resolve any holes or issues in your cover letter:

Be Truthful and Open:
Clearly and honestly acknowledge any gaps or issues in your work history.

Give a succinct justification for the gap, keeping the details minimal and concentrating on the facts.

Pay Attention to the Good:
Highlight the things you performed to maintain productivity or improve your skills throughout the time off.

Emphasize any voluntary labor, independent initiatives, educational endeavors, or pertinent engagements you engaged in over the hiatus.

Comfort Your Employer:
Assure the employer that the absence won't affect your capacity to carry out the job duties.

Talk about your excitement to be back at work and your dedication to the position.

Display Your Transferable Skill Set:

Emphasize in the cover letter any experiences or transferable abilities you have that are pertinent to the role throughout the gap.

Pay attention to how these abilities, despite the lapse in your work experience, make you an attractive prospect.

Keep It Concise:
In a single sentence or brief paragraph, address the gap while emphasizing your qualifications and excitement for the job.

Look for Expert Assistance:
See a career counselor or expert resume writer for guidance if you're unclear on how to handle a particular gap or issue.

For instance:

"I took advantage of the time between jobs to do extra study in digital marketing and earn certifications in Google Analytics and AdWords. With these abilities and my prior experience in conventional marketing roles, I am sure that I am a good contender for the job."

Filling in the blanks and addressing issues in your cover letter shows that you are a proactive, professional, and honest applicant for the position. You can improve your chances of getting the job by doing this and allay any worries the employer might have.

Robert L.White Ph.D

110

CHAPTER 8

RULES AND TIPS FOR SUCCESS

EDITING AND PROOFREADING

It's important to proofread and modify your cover letter to make sure it conveys your qualifications and interest in the job in an error-free, professional manner. To assist you in editing and proofreading your cover letter, follow these steps:

Take a Time Off:

Give your cover letter a break after writing it and then proofread it. This will enable you to view the document from a different perspective.

Read aloud:

Go over your cover letter with a loud voice. This can assist you in spotting typos, strange wording, and grammar mistakes.

Make use of grammar and spell checks:
To identify common mistakes, use the grammar and spell check functions of your word processing program. Don't depend just on these tools, though, as they might miss some errors.

Look for Uniformity:
Make sure that the formatting of your cover letter is consistent throughout, using the same font style, size, and space.

Pay attention to conciseness and clarity:
Ensure that your cover letter is precise, succinct, and direct. Eliminate any words or sentences that are superfluous or contribute nothing of value.

Verify Correctness:
Verify the correctness of all the information you include in your cover letter, including the job title, firm name, and contact details.

Tailor to Every Job Application:
Customize your cover letter for every position you apply for. Verify that it relates to the particular position and business you are applying to.

Request Input:
Get a friend, relative, or coworker to proofread your cover letter. They can offer insightful criticism and point out mistakes you might have missed.

Proofread several times:

Proofread your cover letter more than once, paying attention to distinct details each time (such as spelling, grammar, and formatting). You can identify several error categories with each pass.

Write Professionally:

In your cover letter, use formal language and a professional tone. Don't use jargon, slang, or extremely informal language.

These guidelines will help you make sure your cover letter is error-free, professionally written, and effectively communicates your qualifications and interest in the job.

TOOLS AND TECHNIQUES FOR PROOFREADING

Proofreading is a crucial phase in the writing process that guarantees error-free texts that project a polished, businesslike image. The following resources and methods will help you proofread more effectively:

Make use of grammar and spelling checkers:

To identify common mistakes, use the grammar and spelling checks that come with word processing programs like Google Docs and Microsoft Word.

Read aloud:

Go over your document with yourself out loud. By doing this, you can identify mistakes that you would miss when reading aloud.

Take Breaks
Between writing and editing sessions, take pauses. This can aid in mental renewal and facilitate error detection.

Read Backwards:
Start after your document and read it backward. This can assist you in concentrating on specific words and sentences rather than the meaning as a whole, which will make it simpler to identify mistakes.

Print and Proofread:
Make a hard copy of your document and edit it with a pen and paper. Errors are sometimes simpler to find on paper than they are on screen.

Employ Online Resources:
To find and fix mistakes, use online proofreading resources like Grammarly, ProWritingAid, or Hemingway Editor.

Get People's Opinion:
Get a friend, relative, or coworker to proofread your work. Errors that you might miss are frequently caught by a second pair of eyes.

Employ software for text-to-speech:
If you would like your document read back to you, use text-to-speech software. This might assist you in spotting improper grammar and poor wording.

Check formatting:
Be mindful of formatting elements including alignment, font size, and space. Formatting errors can give the impression that your work is not professional.

Proofread several times:
Proofread your work several times, paying attention to distinct details each time (such as spelling, grammar, and formatting). You can identify several error categories with each pass.

You may raise the standard of your writing and make sure that your publications are polished and devoid of errors by utilizing these tools and strategies.

COMMON RESUME AND COVER LETTER ERRORS
Typical mistakes in a cover letter and resume might hurt your application and decrease your chances of getting an interview. Here are a few typical mistakes to steer avoid:

Resume Mistakes:
Typographical and Grammatical Errors: These can give the impression that you are sloppy and unprofessional. Carefully proofread your resume, or have someone else do so.

Generic Resume: If your resume isn't customized to the position you're seeking, it may not be effective. Make your CV unique for every job by emphasizing your experience and talents that are relevant.

Missing Keywords: Applicant tracking systems (ATS) are widely used by businesses to screen resumes. To improve your chances of getting past the ATS, make sure your resume contains pertinent keywords from the job description.

Absence of Quantifiable Achievements: Your resume will be less effective if it is just a list of your job responsibilities without any emphasis on your accomplishments. Provide measurable accomplishments to prove your worth.

Bad Formatting: A resume with bad formatting might be challenging to understand and may not leave a positive impression. Don't use too many graphics or stylistic elements, and stick to a tidy, businesslike format.

Cover Letter Mistakes
Not Addressing the Hiring Manager: Your cover letter may come across as impersonal if it is not addressed to a specific person. Try to address the hiring manager by name whenever you can.

Being Overly Generic: An employer is unlikely to be impressed by a cover letter that is too general and might be used for any position. Customize your cover letter for the specific position and organization.

Repeating the Content of Your Resume: Your cover letter needs to enhance your resume rather than merely restating its contents. Emphasize parts of your experience that are very pertinent to the position in the cover letter.

Being Excessively Long or Excessively Short: An effective cover letter should be brief and direct. Use your words carefully and try to keep your essay between half and full page in length.

Neglecting to Proofread: Your cover letter should be error-free in grammar and spelling, much like your resume. Before submitting, take the time to carefully proofread it.

You may improve your chances of being noticed by presenting yourself to potential employers more skillfully and avoiding these typical resume and cover letter mistakes.

CHAPTER 9

GUIDELINES FOR DESIGN AND FORMATTING

An effective cover letter is mostly dependent on its layout and design. Here are some pointers to assist you in producing a polished and eye-catching document:

CHOOSING AN APPROPRIATE FONT AND STYLE
Choose a professional and straightforward typeface. Select a simple typeface such as Verdana, Calibri, Arial, or something comparable. Steer clear of ornate or ornamental fonts.

Applicant tracking systems, or software that enables the automated sorting of job applications based on particular keywords, talents, job titles, or other data, are used by many organizations. The software may find it more difficult to read your letter if you choose complicated typefaces, which could stop your application from proceeding.

For easier readability, use 10- and 12-point font sizes. Generally speaking, stick to the font and size selections you made for your resume.

USING BULLET POINTS AND WHITE SPACE EFFECTIVELY

Proper spacing is crucial while writing a cover letter. The hiring manager will find it easy to scan through your letters more quickly if you use white spaces. Observe these rules:

Single-spacing your cover letter is advised.
Every component (contact details, salutation, opening, middle, closing, and complimentary closing) should have a gap added between them. (You do not require any indentation in any of your paragraphs.)
length recommendations.

Your cover letter should consist of three paragraphs and not more than one page. If needed, you can include an additional middle paragraph. However, always ask yourself if you can convey the important information in fewer words before doing this.

Alignment and margins

The text should be aligned to the left and all around with regular 1-inch margins. Read your letter again and see if there are any parts you can cut if it is extending to a second page. If you are unable to make any cuts, think about reducing the margins to 3/4 or 1/2 inch, but don't go any smaller than that.

Format for files

An application tracking system may be processing your cover letter, so be sure you save it in a format that works with it, such as a Word document or PDF. Renaming your file to something more precise is also a good suggestion, particularly since hiring managers can see the file name of your online application. To facilitate the downloader's experience, use the First Name-Last Name-Cover-Letter format (e.g., Jade-Young-cover-letter.doc).

CONCLUSION

Creating a strong CV and cover letter is an essential ability in the competitive job market of today. It's critical to get your resume and cover letter properly because they frequently serve as the prospective employer's initial impression of you. We've covered the guidelines, pointers, and crucial components of creating strong resumes and cover letters throughout this book. We've talked about how crucial it is to customize your materials for every job application, emphasize your accomplishments, and highlight your relevant experiences and talents.

Recall that your CV and cover letter are more than just a summary of your experiences and qualifications as you polish them. These are your chances to present your resume and explain why you are the most qualified applicant for the position. Your resume should highlight your most relevant qualifications clearly and succinctly in a way that is easy to read. Your cover letter should be a supplement to your CV, adding more information, outlining your interest in the role, and outlining how you can help the business succeed.

The value of personalization is among the most important lessons to be learned from this book. Every job is unique, and every company has various requirements in terms of experience and skills. You may demonstrate to employers that you are the ideal candidate for the position and that you understand their demands by customizing your cover letter and resume for each job application.

The choice of language is a crucial component in creating effective cover letters and resumes. Your writing should be error-free and polished. When describing your accomplishments, use action verbs rather than too formal or clichéd phrasing. Make sure you thoroughly proofread your documents before emailing them, because even little mistakes might leave a bad impression on potential employers.

Another crucial step in the job search process is networking. Developing connections with experts in your field might help you find undiscovered employment openings and gain access to businesses that interest you. Never hesitate to ask anyone in your network for guidance or help when you're looking for a job.

To sum up, crafting strong cover letters and resumes is a talent that can be developed with experience. You may improve your chances of getting hired and landing your dream job by heeding the recommendations in this book and making the effort to customize your paperwork for each job application. Don't let rejection deter you from being optimistic and tenacious in your job search. By taking the appropriate approach, you can succeed in your professional endeavors.